AFFIRMING THE HUMAN
AND THE HOLY

AFFIRMING THE HUMAN
AND THE HOLY

PHILOMENA AGUDO, F.M.M., Ph. D.

AFFIRMATION BOOKS
WHITINSVILLE, MASSACHUSETTS

PUBLISHED WITH ECCLESIASTICAL PERMISSION

First Edition
©1979 by House of Affirmation, Inc.

Library of Congress Cataloging in Publication Data
Agudo, Philomena, 1925-
    Affirming the human and the holy.

    1. Psychology, Religious. 2. Personality.
3. Holy, The. I. Title.
BR110.A37   248 '.4   79-1499
ISBN 0-89571-006-4

Printed by Mercantile Printing Company, Worcester, MA
United States of America

To Sr. Anna Polcino, S.C.M.M., M.D.

Who has been a source of healing
and affirmation to many.

CONTENTS

FOREWORD

For several years now I have shared participation in the House of Affirmation therapeutic community with the author of this book, Philomena Agudo. I have come to call her, with affection, "the wise woman from the East." A religious of the Franciscan Missionary Sisters of Mary, an educator, and a doctor of psychology, Philomena Agudo has warmth, charm, friendliness, scholarship, and deep religious convictions that echo her Philippine origins.

Affirming the Human and the Holy is a series of reflections wherein the author invites her readers to ponder the tremendous potential they have within themselves to develop as fully human and fully holy persons. Doctor Agudo chooses to emphasize the unique role of affirmation in reference to the self while not getting lost in the futility of self-affirmation. In many ways, this book serves as a guide in the Christian's search for God through an awareness of the self.

Sister Philomena has made an important contribution to literature in the field of psychotheology. While her book is not meant to be an exhaustive study, or a full explanation of developmental psychology or spiritual formation, it does point out a way of discovering the sacredness in humanity. Sister Philomena draws from her own integrated life as a woman of science, a woman of theology, and a woman of prayer.

All psychotherapists must ultimately be measured by their respect for the individual, their personal integrity, and their self-understanding as reflected in their own life styles. The extent to which a psychotherapist has integrated his or her own psychological and spiritual growth will influence a client's opportunity for healing. As Karl Jasper has insisted: "The therapist is the patient's fate." The author brings to her clients a deep sense of respect for the individual, as so well evidenced in these chapters.

I wish to thank Sister Philomena for allowing Affirmation Books to present her ideas to the general public. I recommend *Affirming the Human and the Holy* for careful consideration and prayerful reflection.

Thomas A. Kane, Ph.D., D.P.S.
Priest, Diocese of Worcester
International Executive Director
House of Affirmation

January 3, 1979

PREFACE

There were times in the past when humanistic philosophy was looked upon with suspicion and even condemnation. Such an attitude brought with it an impression that being human was wrong and even sinful. It seemed then that God made a mistake in creating human beings! As a consequence, religious formation was geared to a sort of "angelic perfection"—an unrealistic goal.

One need only reflect on the Gospels to grasp a predominant theme—Christ's consistent affirmation of the human and the holy. The Pharisees were obsessed with being perfect and rejected what was human through their compulsive rituals and legalism. They were unaware that in rejecting the human they also rejected the holy.

Modern society has fostered a certain permissiveness that is also a rejection of the holy and a desecration of the human person. The denial of either the human or the holy in the person results in the gradual deterioration of the personality. The person becomes disoriented, emotionally disturbed, and confused.

Personality wholeness is possible only when there is an unconditional acceptance and integration of both the human and the sacred elements in the person. This book does not presume to offer an easy means to attain such an integration. It is a humble attempt to share with the reader some reflections based on clinical experience.

I am profoundly grateful to the residents of the House of Affirmation who permitted me to reproduce their paintings in this book. Their courage to accept themselves has enabled them to create works of art out of their sufferings. I also wish to express my sincere appreciation to the former and present residents whose lives are a continual proof of the transcendence of the human spirit; to Lynnette Perry for her patience in editing the manuscripts and in preparing the book for publication; and, finally, to Dr. Anna Polcino and Rev. Dr. Thomas A. Kane for their unfailing encouragement.

We need to get in touch with our
inmost core—the self, upon which
all relationships depend.

I

THE CORE OF THE HUMAN

As we journey through life, we are sooner or later confronted with the phenomenon of individual freedom. We discover the major role choice plays in our lives. We are equally free to allow past negative and traumatic experiences to cripple our personalities or to seek the help necessary to bring about growth and healing. In short, we are free to affirm or reject ourselves.

The self is the core of the person's being. It is the personality center. Through the self, the individual becomes aware of his or her uniqueness, identity, and worth. The self enables the person to perceive reality in a certain manner and to interpret it. The self formulates the person's values and shapes his or her attitudes toward life. Since the self is the organizational center of the personality, it determines and regulates the person's behavior patterns. When so determining and regulating, the self is free to choose the constructive or destructive manner of responding to people and situations.

It is the nature of the self to discover the meaning of its existence. It strives to understand its experiences and to organize them into meaningful wholes.[1] The person is able to discover meaning in his or her existence only because of his or her free will. The person is free to choose the particular meaning of his or her life.[2]

The self innately desires integration. Its direction is toward goals and fulfillment. The self strives for actualization. F. C. Thorne considers the primary motive in life to be "self-enhancement on all levels of integration."[3]

The self has a transcendent character, a quality that "renders man a being reaching out beyond himself."[4] This transcendent character enables the person to rise above the fetters of heredity, culture, and the tragic situations in life. Because persons have this capacity for transcendence, they are able to change and reshape their own characters.

DEVELOPMENT OF SELF-CONCEPT

The foundation for the development of a person's self-concept is laid during the first two years after birth. Elizabeth Hurlock calls babyhood the "critical period,"[5] for

---

1. C. H. Patterson, *Theories of Counseling and Psychotherapy* (New York: Harper and Row, 1973), p. 468.
2. Viktor Frankl, *The Will to Meaning* (New York: New American Library, 1969), p. 16.
3. F. C. Thorne, *Integrative Psychology* (Brandon, VT: Clinical Psychology Publishing Co., 1967), p. vii.
4. Frankl, p. 16.
5. Elizabeth Hurlock, *Developmental Psychology* (New York: McGraw-Hill, 1959), pp. 552; 538.

during this time a person's basic adult personality structure develops. The individual may not remember what happened during these years, but his or her experiences as a baby are vitally important in the formation of self-concept. The person's self-image has its beginnings in the limited confines of the home in which the parent-child relationships evolve during the period of babyhood.

In early childhood (two to six years), personality development occurs as the child becomes aware of his or her world, perceives people and situations, and relates to them. The child internalizes how people think and feel about him or her; thus the child's self-image develops from the manner in which he or she is being treated by his or her parents and other family members.

During late childhood (six years to the onset of puberty), the child's self-concept undergoes frequent revisions. The child first sees himself or herself through the eyes of his or her parents; as the child goes to school, teachers, classmates, and neighbors comprise the people who further the development of the child's self-image. The child's attitude toward himself or herself is dependent on the attitudes of parents, teachers, siblings, and peers. If the treatment of the child manifests appreciation and love, the child will have a healthy self-image; but when deprived of emotional nourishment, the child learns to devalue or even reject himself or herself.

In early adolescence, the individual is aware of his or her good and bad traits. He or she also becomes aware of how his or her personality affects relationship to others. If the adolescent feels that others find likeable qualities in him or her, the adolescent will be able to make satisfactory social adjustment; but if the adolescent's self-image is dependent wholly upon others' attitudes, then self-alienation is a dangerous possibility. The self-alienated adolescent will try to please others and strive to fulfill impossible expectations in order to gain acceptance.

Late adolescence is a most dangerous period in the development of self-concept because its negative experiences will likely influence the individual's adult personality pattern. The person who believes he or she is regarded by others favorably begins to accept himself or herself. If, on the contrary, a person believes that others regard him or her unfavorably, that person's resulting negativistic self-image will cause the person to reject his or her authentic self. Such a negative self-concept manifests itself in personal and social maladjustments.

In early adulthood, adjustment to the problems of adult life affects the self-concept of the individual. Successful adjustment results in increased self-confidence and an inner sense of security. Failures in adjustment, however, result in feelings of inadequacy and inferiority. Self-concept remains stable throughout the adult years and becomes more fixed with age unless an unexpected, marked change occurs. Any change in self-concept is possible only because of the transcendent quality of the self.

With middle age, the individual experiences changes in appearance, competency, and roles. These changes affect the person's self-concept; so the person must then revise his or her self-image. During this period, the person must accept himself or herself totally in order to make a successful adjustment to changes in life and to prepare for the reality of the aging process.

In old age, the individual's self-concept is greatly influenced by the manner in which he or she is treated by the social group. The treatment received from society will be reflected in his or her behavior. Thus negative social attitudes toward elderly persons result in negative behavior. However, a person who has developed self-acceptance through the years may be able to adjust satisfactorily to the aging process. Adjusting to aging implies accepting the limitations of age. Hurlock explains: "Unfavorable attitudes toward self, other people, work, and life in general can lead to senility just as changes in the brain tissue can."[6] The elderly person who is depressed and disorganized is usually the person who failed to develop any other interests in life after retirement.

According to R. T. Watson, "a person is as old as his self-concept."[7] Changes in personality during old age are caused by change in an individual's self-concept. The disdain for age that is common in youth can be a contributing factor in a person's poor self-concept in old age. Yet when the seeds of self-acceptance have been allowed to flourish through the years, a person's resulting positive self-concept will enable him or her to face the closing years of life with greater peace and satisfaction.

THE REAL SELF

Every human person has the capacity to accept or reject himself or herself. Every individual has a "real self" and an "ideal self." Which of the two a person decides to accept will determine the kind of personality he or she will develop. Karen Horney speaks of the real self as "that cen-

---

6. Ibid., p. 358.
7. R. T. Watson, "The Personality of the Aged," *Journal of Gerontology* 9 (1954): 309-15.

tral inner force, common to all human beings and yet unique in each, which is the deep source of growth.''[8] The real self includes the innate gifts, potentials, and limitations of the person; it also comprises the person's feelings, capacity to express them, willpower, and ability to make decisions and relate to others. The real self is the person's "basic inner reality; the actual feelings, wishes, thoughts, memories, and fantasies . . . as these arise spontaneously.''[9] The real self is not static. It goes through a process of change, a course of evolution as growth takes place in the individual. According to Horney, the real self is the "original force toward individual growth and fulfillment.''[10]

Personality integration is possible only when the person is in touch with his or her real self. When an individual is spontaneously in touch with his or her feelings so that he or she is able to make decisions, be responsible for them, and accept their consequences, that individual manifests an integrated and authentic identity.

The person who accepts his or her real self is able to formulate accurate beliefs about his or her own "modal inner experience.''[11] Such a person experiences ideals and values as his or her own, and expectations of the self lie within the limits of his or her capabilities. He or she is not perpetually

8. Karen Horney, *Neurosis and Human growth* (New York: W. W. Norton, 1950), p. 17.
9. S. M. Jourard, *Personal Adjustment* (New York: Macmillan, 1968), p. 155.
10. Karen Horney, *The Collected Works of Karen Horney,* vol. 2 (New York: W. W. Norton, 1952), p. 158.
11. Jourard, p. 157.

on the defensive, is honest, and is interested in the truth with regard to his or her authentic self.

THE IDEAL SELF

Horney describes the ideal self as "what we are in our irrational imagination, or what we should be according to the dictates of neurotic pride."[12] The ideal self has an insatiable hunger for perfection. Since perfection is certainly not a part of the real self, the individual tends to reject the reality of imperfection in himself or herself. The individual clings tenaciously to the ideal self and is consequently held by the fetters of how he or she "should" act and not how he or she honestly wants to act. The individual sets for the self ideals and values that are impossible for the self to attain. The person also establishes inaccurate beliefs about and images of himself or herself to the point that, when unable to attain the standards by which he or she expects to gain acceptance, the person is crushed by feelings of guilt and failure. The individual then compulsively tries to please people and abides by his or her unattainable standards regardless of real feelings or wishes, for fear of rejection, guilt, and anxiety.

How do we get into the tangles of the ideal self? A healthy emotional environment is necessary for an individual to be in touch with the development of his or her own real self. A child may grow up in the midst of non-accepting adults, dominating and overexacting parents who, unaware, set impossible standards of perfection for

12. Horney, *The Collected Works*, p. 158.

the child to attain. Love, the emotional nourishment of the child, is given by these adults on the condition that the child achieve, succeed, and behave acceptably according to standards imposed by the family. The child is not given the chance to be his or her real self—to fail, make mistakes, blunder in behavior and judgment, love and hate at times, and be both submissive and rebellious. The child absorbs the ideal self from the standards set by his or her parents and other adults in the environment. In the child's effort and desire to be accepted, he or she formulates the "shoulds" that become the basis of his or her personality. The "shoulds," however, become the ruling tyrants of life, which is consequently dominated by intense anxiety, guilt, and fear of rejection. The child develops into either a compliant or an aggressive individual. As a child, the conforming individual subordinates himself or herself to others, becomes emotionally dependent on others, and always tries to be unselfish and good to please others. When a child, the aggressive individual places great value on strength and his or her capacity to endure and fight for survival. The emotions internalized are those of anger, hostility, and hate. Because of the deprivation of emotional nourishment, he or she has no chance to develop the capacity to love. The ideal self of the compliant as well as of the aggressive individual blocks the process of integration.

The ideal self also prevents the development of self-confidence, for the individual gains his or her sense of security only in being accepted by others. He or she has not learned to believe in himself or herself or to trust his or her own abilities because he or she continually sets standards of behavior that are beyond his or her power to attain.

MOVING AWAY FROM AND
AGAINST THE REAL SELF

As the person focuses his or her energies on the ideal self, he or she moves away from and against his or her real self. Horney calls this action "alienation from self." The individual refuses to accept his or her true feelings, beliefs, and wishes in favor of the impossible, or the ideal. Feelings of anger are not recognized or accepted because they are "improper" according to the individual's standards. The individual cannot weep to express loss or grief because weeping would manifest "weakness." Every time the individual is confronted by his or her own mistakes or failure, he or she experiences self-rejection because he or she is unable to accept such human limitations. A person thus alienated from his or her real self becomes depersonalized.[13]

The effects of self-alienation can easily be detected in overemotionalism, overenthusiasm, or discouragement that comes too consistently. The person is easily incited to love or anger, but these emotions are without depth. The person lives in a world of imagination and responds superficially to situations that confront him or her. Such a person has a deep need to impress people.[14]

Some self-alienated persons may even give the appearance of emotional strength, taking risks such as intrigues, sexual acting out, reckless driving, or other dare-devil performances. This need for excitement and thrill are indications of an inner vacuum that is both painful and anxiety

---

13. Horney, *Neurosis and Human Growth,* p. 161.
14. Ibid, pp. 161-62; 164-65.

provoking. These persons need continually to prove something to themselves. They have never integrated the intellect and the emotions and as a result have experienced personality fragmentation. Because of this absence of unity or integration, a substitute control system must hold together the disintegrated parts. Such persons find it more convenient to intellectualize or rationalize than to be in touch with their feelings. They try to live only through the intellectualization of situations and the negation of their emotions. They face one conflict after another while trapped in continual anxiety.

Sr. Barbara Marie Palicki

Affirming the self implies a deep appreciation for life and a continuing sense of gratitude for the experiences life brings.

II

AFFIRMING THE SELF

The behavior of an emotionally autonomous individual is greatly different from that of a person who finds satisfaction in dependency. The dependent person has some degree of immaturity and gauges his or her self-worth according to other people's opinions and expectations. The dependent person exhibits a compulsion to please and an obsessive fear of rejection. The dependent person is self-alienated. He or she has not come to terms with the core of his or her being. Such a person experiences a continual vacuum within, an intense emptiness and loneliness. Conforming to the group becomes this person's means of achieving feelings of security. Thus the dependent person's happiness comes from outside the self. Since a dependent person's happiness is determined by the presence or approval of others, that person is perpetually plagued by anxiety.

The autonomous person, on the other hand, has learned to affirm himself or herself. Like the psalmist, the autonomous person is able to profess the reality of his or her being:

> You, Lord, are all I have,
>   and you give me all I need;
> How wonderful are your gifts to me;
>   how good they are. (Ps. 16: 5-6)

REALITY AND THE SELF

Affirmation of the self is the acknowledgement and the appreciation of one's real self. Perception of reality is relative with regard to an individual's being. A person's perception of self could be accurate or inaccurate. Self-hate as well as self-rejection can affect a person's perception of reality, exaggerating, distorting, and misinterpreting it. A person who has rejected the self perceives other people as rejecting. An individual who has never developed trust or loyalty to the self will be suspicious of others and incapable of loyalty.

The individual who accepts the real self is able to perceive reality more accurately. Accurate perception of self implies the acknowledgement of one's limitations as well as one's gifts and potential. Self-knowledge facilitates effective adjustment to situations and people. It is self-awareness that enables us to make responsible choices with regard to our behavior and reactions. Persons who have affirmed the self have the ability to accept and cope with the here and now. They do not use the past as an excuse for an unfulfilled life; their experiences, no matter how traumatic, are not allowed to be crippling instruments. Failures and disappointments are not allowed to be catastrophes but become learning and growth experiences.

FEELINGS AND EMOTIONS

Situational reality may not be easy to deny for some persons, but, oftentimes, the reality of emotions is distorted and negated. The capacity to feel is one of the functions of the self. Rejection of one's feelings is rejection of one's self. Affirming the self implies listening to the self, listening to the flutterings of joy and the intensity of pain. Such interior communication enables the person to choose the appropriate means by which to express feelings in a mature and constructive manner. Common sense and good judgment are necessary for an individual to decide when and how to express emotions appropriately. One is aware of one's common sense, or intuitive wisdom, only when one habitually experiences self-communication. Martin Buber explains why self-communication is so important:

> . . . The man who experiences has no part in the world. For it is "in him" and not between him and the world that the experience arises.
>
> The world has no part in the experience. It permits itself to be experienced, but has no concern in the matter. For it does nothing to the experience, and the experience does nothing to it.[1]

Emotionally dependent persons tend to habitually suppress their feelings. They so hunger for acceptance and love that they dare not express any negative feelings for fear of rejection. Children who are quiet, passive, and overly submissive have learned to suppress their feelings because they are aware that they are loved only on condition that they adhere to the standards of behavior set by adults. Such prolonged emotional suppression, however,

---

1. Martin Buber, *I and Thou,* trans. Ronald Gregor Smith (New York: Scribner's, 1958), p. 5.

results in explosive outbursts that hinder the development of an integrated personality.

FREEDOM

> Man is never fully conditioned in the sense of being determined by any facts or forces. Rather man is ultimately self-determining—determining not only his fate but even his own self for man is not only forming and shaping the course of his life but also his very self.[2]

The person who has an affirmed self is aware of such a freedom. The greatest gift bestowed upon every human person is the freedom to make choices. When a person is deprived of the right to make decisions, he or she is degraded. When an individual refuses to make decisions for fear of being blamed, he or she manifests immaturity and dependency.

A child with overprotective parents is deprived of developing an autonomous and healthy personality. Overprotective surroundings draw a person to authoritarian structures wherein dependency is reinforced and the desire for autonomy is crushed. Conformity for the sake of acceptance prevents the individual from independent thought and critical evaluation. The individual feels guilty and disloyal when he or she finds some rules or regulations questionable. Structures and authority figures thus inhibit growth toward maturity.

The affirmed individual respects and appreciates his or her freedom to determine as well as to achieve goals in life. Moreover, he or she is aware that finding fulfillment in life depends on how the gift of freedom is used and that free-

---

2. Viktor Frankl, "Dynamics, Existence and Values," *Journal of Existential Psychiatry* 2 (1961): 6.

dom can be used either for growth toward self-fulfillment or for self-destruction.

RESPONSIBILITY

> . . . man is not only responsible for what he does but also for what he is, inasmuch as man does not only behave according to what he is but also becomes according to how he behaves. In the last analysis, man has become what he has made out of himself. Instead of being fully conditioned by any conditions he is rather constructing himself.[3]

One important characteristic of an integrated personality is the person's sense of responsibility. The integrated person affirms his or her freedom to make choices and is responsible for those choices. He or she is able to accept both the positive and negative consequences and use them for growth and fulfillment. Blaming the past, parents, structures, or the environment points to irresponsibility. Some factors are beyond the individual's control, but the person is free to make the best of the situation. Giving in to frustration or despair simply means that the person does not want to be responsible, does not care what happens to the self. Being irresponsible is the same as being self-destructive. One has to be responsible for one's physical and mental health. One must exert every effort to attain the maturity and integration that are essential factors in leading a meaningful and purposeful life.

If the human body, or life itself, is a gift from God, the person has responsibility to take special care of that gift. To neglect the human body or to hate it would be a viola-

---

3. Ibid.

tion of the divine law. In fact, a simple definition of sin is behavior that tends to destroy oneself and others.

The innate freedom in us makes us capable of either affirming or destroying ourselves. Human history is replete with suicides, murders, and wars. Every human being is continually pulled between the tendency to build or to destroy, to choose life or death. If God has indeed endowed us with free will, why did he have to impose his commandments? The commandments of God reflect his compassion. They were set down to protect us from destruction.

LOVE OF SELF

The capacity to love oneself measures one's capacity to love God and others. A person who cannot love himself or herself discovers that God is distant and threatening as well as punitive and that satisfying relationships with others are unattainable. In the past, love of self was erroneously associated with the sin of pride. The reality is that it takes great love of self to avoid sin (destructive behavior) and to attain eternal salvation (ultimate self-fulfillment). I have often met persons who prefer to be alone because being with others does not give them satisfaction, who cannot pray because they believe God does not really love but punishes. These very same persons often admit to hating themselves, to wishing they were dead, or to fantasizing the means by which to kill themselves. They have not learned to love the gift of self.

Love of self is appreciation and respect for one's being, including one's personal history, race, sexual identity, physical appearance, and culture. An autonomous individual is able to withstand criticisms or unfavorable remarks. That person's autonomy has been possible because deep within the individual lies self-trust and self-loyalty. Love of self also includes self-honesty, or being true to oneself, with no pretensions, masks, or phoniness to impress others. It was for phoniness and hypocrisy that Christ condemned the Pharisees:

> How accurately Isaiah prophesied about you hypocrites when he wrote:
>> "This people pays me lip service
>> but their heart is far from me.
> Empty is the reverence they do me
> because they teach as dogmas mere
> human precepts."
> You disregard God's commandment and·cling to what is human tradition.   (Mark 7:6-8)

The individual who is true to self does not feel the compulsive need to impress others. Self-acceptance takes priority over social approval. The individual appreciates his or her freedom from the compulsion to conform unquestioningly. The person believes in his or her convictions because the person believes in himself or herself. Affirming the self deepens one's intimacy with the self, which in turn brings about the ability to relate personally and closely with God, family, and friends.

We can never ignore the holy in ourselves. Either we come to terms with it and integrate it into our being or we reject it and bring about our own destruction.

III

THE HOLY IN THE HUMAN

Evil in the human has long been overemphasized. To encounter it, we need only read newspapers, novels, and poetry and watch television. Yet human evil is only part of reality. The holy is also present in the human and has never been proportionately and sufficiently extolled or appreciated. The individual who is able to recognize and appreciate the holy in himself or herself transcends human limitations and comes in contact with God.

THE SELF AND GRACE

Wilfried Daim believes that man's constitutional design points to the True Absolute and that attachment to a false absolute brings about a disorientation of the personality center that could result in mental derangement. He points to the need for "salvation."[1] The human need for salvation is described as "a state of restlessness, of being unfulfilled and unsatisfied."[2] The person experiencing helplessness, anxiety, and insecurity feels in desperate need for help from an omnipotent Being. The source of this transcendent help is God, and we identify the supernatural help as grace. Daim explains:

> . . . man's basic constitutional design points toward God, that is, toward an infinite end. And only such a being-ordained toward an infinite God can there be freedom. Contrariwise, there must be compulsion in any finite anthropological system because the basically overt organization of man is bound to hit against the walls of finitude.
> The cause then of the compulsive nature, of fixation is the finiteness of the absolutized entity.[3]

Human development is essentially intertwined with the holy. Emotional growth is possible only because the human and the holy are allowed to interact and are integrated. Daim states: "God endows nature with its own free development. Only an actual infinite love object of the heart guarantees free growth."[4]

---

1. Wilfried Daim, *Depth Psychology and Salvation,* trans. and ed. Kurt Reinhardt (New York: Frederick Ungar, 1963), p. 33.
   Wilfried Daim is a Catholic Austrian psychiatrist. His theory maintains that a person afflicted with "fixation" is attached to a "false absolute" that causes suffering and creates in the person a "need for salvation."
2. Ibid.
3. Ibid., p. 44.
4. Wilfried Daim, "Depth Psychology and Grace," trans. Cornelie Ernst, *Journal of Psychotherapy and Religious Process* 1 (1954): 34.

Being human means having a tendency toward an absolute. This tendency is so because of human finiteness. Absolutes, however, are either false or true. False absolutes turn out to be tyrannical idols that disappoint, frustrate, and cause conflicts and restlessness within the individual. These idols are clearly illustrated in the Old Testament. False absolutes never give peace. Daim describes that fundamental drive aiming toward the true Absolute-God:

> The tendency towards the true Absolute is a dynamic principle; it is impulsive, driving and forceful. . . . This fundamental drive, entelechially aiming towards God, is the deepest drive in man's soul and identical with the self.[5]

Communication and relationship with the true Absolute, however, depend upon the person's attitude toward himself or herself. Acceptance and love of self open the whole being to God's grace. Rejection and hatred of self close the communication with God and push the individual toward false absolutes that bring about self-destruction rather than growth. Persons who cannot pray and who believe that God is distant and unreal have never learned to affirm themselves and, unfortunately, are unaware of their own self-rejection and self-hatred. As such persons progress in therapy and gradually develop a degree of self-appreciation, they are able to pray and to celebrate their communion with God.

---

5. Ibid.

PSYCHOTHERAPY AND GRACE

Psychotherapy, a human function, parallels and is complemented by the holy function of grace. Daim was clearly convinced of this parallel when he wrote:

> . . . The intentions of actual grace and psychotherapy are fundamentally similar, although they become effective at two different points. While grace strengthens, furthers and kindles the fundamental drive of man's soul towards God and thus induces man to intensify his struggle against fixations, psychotherapy primarily works against the fixations to free nature. . . . It is capable only of removing fixations, not of helping nature or accelerating the fundamental vitality of the heart. . . .
>
> Grace now is a positive force, intensifying the fundamental vitality of the heart and "inspiring" as related in the prayer.[6]

The reality of the human and the holy in the individual enables psychotherapy to work toward grace. The removal of fixations and the emotional growth that results in the development of self-esteem open the individual to grace. Psychotherapy without grace is an incomplete process. The human element may be nourished by psychotherapy, but unless psychotherapy prepares the individual for the holy, i.e., grace, wholeness in the person can never be achieved. Daim explains:

> Actual grace strengthens the driving forces of the heart and also the fundamental conflict of human nature in a supernatural way, while psychotherapy removes fixations and concentrates on the natural forces within the heart. True psychotherapy, therefore, takes the road towards grace.[7]

6. Ibid., p. 39.
7. Ibid., p. 40.

SELF-ALIENATION AND IDOLATRY

The self-alienated person is usually immersed in self-hate. Such a person experiences emptiness and void within to the point that he or she frantically grasps at false absolutes to fill the vacuum. These false absolutes symbolize acceptance or love, but they serve only to heighten anxiety rather than to reassure the person, to thicken the walls of the neurotic prison rather than to bestow freedom upon the individual. Daim describes the result:

> Since he is enslaved by an idol, a false absolute, he does not take God as the model for his actions, but the idol, the orders and demands of which are really binding ones for him. Those demands by virtue of their absolute character take over the task of conscience. They are compulsive because they are not in keeping with the true nature of man, to whom they are directed. The demands of the unknown idol terrorize man's nature which is really suited to the proper demands of conscience. The idol's demands are irrational, in spite of the fact that again and again the attempt is made to give them a rational appearance. Freud calls it "rationalization," Adler "arrangement." Underneath lies true nature of man which tries to force its way through the layer of coercion—that is the fixation—out into freedom.[8]

Fixation, which is false absolutism, imprisons the individual in his or her neurosis. The person thus imprisoned desires in his or her true nature to be liberated. The holy within, which is the conscience, inspires the person to seek the true center—the true Absolute. The freedom achieved through the human process of psychotherapy brings about

---

8. Ibid., p. 108.

the freedom *from* idols and false absolutes and the freedom *toward* the source of the holy—God.

FALSE ABSOLUTES OF DESPAIR, INFERIORITY, AND HOSTILITY

Three predominant feelings consistently stand out in the mentally or emotionally disturbed person: the pervasive feelings of despair, inferiority, and hostility. The individual in despair has a deep hatred of self. He or she thus embraces an idol or a false god. When this idol does not produce peace or harmony within, the individual finds life meaningless and wants to destroy himself or herself. Daim considers such action a revolt against grace:

> Despair implies . . . pride and arrogance deriving from an indignant revolt against the actually demanded dependency on grace. This is, as a matter of fact amounts to, a revolt against salvation as such . . . despair always includes the elements of impatience and revolt as well as a lack of faith, hope and love. Despair in short is essentially an unwillingness to believe in saving grace.[9]

Feelings of inferiority are symptomatic of self-rejection. Such feelings surface when an individual has failed to develop self-esteem and an inner sense of security, which stem from centering on the True Absolute. This inferiority complex is also indicative of immaturity. Persons who are age fifty chronologically but age five emotionally are not unusual. Feelings of inferiority are another manifestation of fixation. Daim states:

> The person who remains inflexibly attached to a specific stage of human growth, exhibits in his infan-

9. Daim, *Depth Psychology and Salvation*, p. 59.

tility a lack of maturity of the later phases of personal development. . . . the person remains "stuck" and cannot attain to a full flowering of his essential nature.[10]

Fixation or idolization causes an individual to perceive reality inaccurately. Inaccurate perception of situations and persons makes the individual hostile toward self and others. Daim discusses the effects of idolization:

> . . . idolization also lies at the root or prepares the soil for dissension, division and discord among individuals—among human beings who have surrendered their selves to an illusory pseudo reality, a reality which appears in a different light to each of them and which engenders perpetual struggles and quarrels. . . . Idolization carries in its wake disintegration as a derivative modality.[11]

THE SELF AND LIBERATION FROM FIXATIONS

Affirming the self begins with the realization that the self at one stage has developed a certain form of fixation. The idol could be the father, the mother, or any member of the family. The human needs salvation. Salvation is possible only when the individual accepts his or her need to be liberated from inhibiting idols. It involves the attainment of personal autonomy from controling relations. Liberation from human fixations, however, is not possible through human efforts alone. Salvation is a state achieved through the integrating forces of both the human and the holy. Daim describes the role of the Savior:

> . . . the Savior therefore, must be a created being, and since man occupies the highest rank among beings of

---

10. Ibid., p. 85.
11. Ibid., p. 136.

visible creation, and since man has a share in the entire hierarchy of beings of created nature, the Savior must have a share in the humanity of man. Only by being both God and man will he be able to respond to the need and want of human nature. Since the fixations dominate the world to such an extent that it cannot free itself unaided, the Savior must himself be free from the shackles of fixation. . . . It is this freedom from fixation which imparts to the Savior the inner possibility to liberate.[12]

The Savior takes upon himself the resistance, the hostility, and the negativism of the individual to be saved. He exposes himself to these destructive forces in order to accomplish the individual's salvation. Consequently, all healing power, including psychotherapy, has its "root principle in Christ."[13]

---

12. Ibid., p. 275
13. Ibid.

Identity involves listening to self.
Only then do we become aware
of our personhood, our gifts,
and our limitations.

IV

IDENTITY—LISTENING TO
THE HUMAN AND THE HOLY

The process of identification in childhood is a very important stage in personality development. Since the object of identification is a human being, the reality of imperfection has to be faced. During the teen years, a girl or a boy struggles with his or her identity and has an innate desire to be his or her own person. When adults either refuse to affirm this struggle or expect conformity, the boy or girl will either rebel or deny his or her self-identity. When the boy or girl grows to adulthood, he or she will then be indecisive, without personal convictions, and too anxious about other people's impressions or opinions. In short, the boy or girl will be alienated from his or her real self.

Why are some adults deprived of self-identity? Abraham Maslow states that "the greatest cause of our alienation from our real selves is our neurotic involvements with other people, the historical hangovers from childhood, the irrational transferences, in which past and present are confused, and in which the adult acts like a child."[1] Personal autonomy is necessary for the achievement of self-identity, and Christ made personal autonomy a condition necessary for the achievement of Christian maturity.[2]

IDENTITY AND MEANING

Paradoxically, adults attain self-identity not by self-analysis, but by listening to their intuition of commitment. According to Viktor Frankl, a person finds identity only to the extent that "he commits himself to something beyond himself, to a cause greater than himself."[3] In every human being there is a desire for commitment—to a person or to a cause. Individuals are able to appreciate their identity as worthwhile only when they are committed to others or to a cause that is beyond the human. As we look at different cultures and races through the ages, a pattern of commitment to an omnipotent being as well as to a supernatural cause recurs. Communism's attempt to wipe out religion simultaneously destroys personal identity.

Commitment gives meaning to a person's life. Only when an individual has found a real meaning to his or her existence is he or she able to appreciate his or her true identity.

1. Abraham Maslow, *The Farther Reaches of Human Nature* (New York: Viking Press, 1972), p. 65.
2. Matt. 10:37.
3. Viktor Frankl, *Psychotherapy and Existentialism* (New York: Simon and Schuster, 1967), p. 9.

IDENTITY AND CREATIVITY

Creativity, according to Silvano Arieti, is a prerogative of man; it can be seen as the humble human counterpart of God's creation.[4] Traditionally, creativity was considered to be the birthright of geniuses. But every human being has a certain degree of creativity, of originality that needs to be recognized, used, and appreciated. Just as each plant is endowed with a biological power to produce leaves and stems, every human individual is gifted with a unique potential that, when acknowledged, affirms that individual's identity. Human beings possess a transcendent quality of will and freedom that enables them to either develop their potential or let it stagnate through life.

Arieti quotes P. Matussek: "Creativity does not depend on inherited talent or on environment or upbringing; it is the function of the ego of every human being."[5] Originality or creativity does not happen magically. The individual is free to will creativity and to develop the potential with which he or she is endowed. Thomas Edison was a failure in algebra and was considered a slow learner, but these setbacks did not deter him from recognizing his gifts. Albert Einstein admitted that, as he examined himself and his methods of thought, he came to the conclusion that the gift of fantasy had meant more to him than his talent for absorbing knowledge.[6] He appreciated his power to fantasize. Fantasies have often been associated with the per-

---

4. Silvano Arieti, *Creativity: The Magic Synthesis* (New York: Basic Books, 1976), p. 4.
5. Ibid., p. 10.
6. R. W. Clark, *Einstein: The Life and Times* (New York: World), p. 87.

son's desire to escape from realities of life. Einstein was able to perceive the positive side of his fantasies. They gave the clue to his potential and established his identity.

GRATITUDE

Gratitude, always considered a virtue, can also be a conditioned behavior. Its sincerity and depth are intimately linked with personal identity. An individual's capacity to be sincerely grateful is a function of that person's appreciation and gratitude for his or her own being and self-worth. A person who has not achieved a solid acceptance of his or her identity finds it very difficult to appreciate the behavior of others, much less to appreciate his or her own existence. Appreciation of self results in a habitual attitude of gratitude for what one is, for what one has, and for one's positive interaction with others. Appreciation and gratitude for one's identity enables one to be open to a more personal relationship with one's Creator, one's Savior. In other words, a person is open to the workings of grace only when he or she has a deep sense of appreciation for his or her identity.

THE CAPACITY TO LOVE AND TO HATE

The capacity to experience and express both positive and negative feelings begins with the identification of the child with either parent. If the process of identification has followed its normal course, and the child has had adequate emotional nourishment of love and affection from both parents, the girl identifies herself with her mother and gradually appreciates her femininity as she grows toward adolescence and young adulthood. The boy, in turn, feeling secure in his father's love, looks up to his father as his model for his masculine identity. By appreciating his father, he develops an esteem for his masculinity. Appreciation and love for one's sexual identity becomes the foundation and basis for the capacity to love. Love of others is rooted in love of self. Even the capacity to love God begins with self-esteem, which is in reality a sincere gratitude for the gift of one's being and existence.

The capacity to hate develops similarly when, instead of being given emotional nourishment, the child is either deprived of love and affection or is traumatized by cruelty from either parent. Children who grow up in a hostile environment in which they witness cruelty and violence become aggressive or suicidal persons. Why has the Middle East become the breeding ground for terrorists? After World War II, the refugee Palestinians continued to live in tents not fit for human beings. In such inhuman conditions, parents are not able to give love or affection to their children since they themselves are immersed in bitterness and resentment over their plight. Since they had no country of their own, no decent dwelling place to call their own, the refugees and their children had no chance to develop a sense of appreciation for their identity. The struggle for survival and the attendant frustrations crushed tender feelings and developed instead the capacity to hate and destroy.

When children internalize hatred from their parents or their environment, they develop a hatred for themselves. Because they lack self-esteem, they are unable to establish satisfactory relationships with anyone. Their capacity to hate is turned not only toward themselves but toward others as well. Thus sexual perversion and aggression can be traced to the rejection of self-identity.

The capacity to love as a religious, as a priest, as a wife and mother, and as a husband and father is a function of one's acceptance and love of one's sexual identity. When Christ gave his commandment of love, he based it on the love of self, which implies the affirmation of one's personal identity.

Michael

Our sense of values ennobles our
human personality. Without it,
we regress into patterns of ani-
malistic survival.

V

VALUES—THE HOLY
UPLIFTING THE HUMAN

Individuals who are uncertain about personal values often experience an identity crisis. They fail to achieve wholeness or integration either because they are unable or they refuse to differentiate between what is constructive and destructive, right and wrong, good and evil. Devoid of values, such persons live without any sense of direction and therefore find human existence meaningless and confusing.

A sense of values has its beginnings within the family. Peers, education, personal experiences, and personal reflections contribute to a formulation of values that the individual adheres to throughout life. The spiritual dimension of the human person is integrated into an individual's personality only when that individual possesses values and adheres to them.

THE ROOT OF HUMAN VALUES

If there is any consistent pattern in the lives of saints, it is the persistent adherence to personal values. Such adherence is clearly manifested in the lives of the fisherman, Peter; the poor man, Francis of Assissi; the warrior, Joan of Arc; and the farm girl, Maria Goretti. St. Thomas Aquinas (*Summa Theologica,* I-II, 9:2) points to man's "participation in the eternal design," which illucidates every human person's relationship with the Creator regardless of whether he or she accepts or denies the existence of such a relationship. Human existence is self-transcendent because man's primary concern is not limited to self-actualization, but includes the realization of values. Values acquire their objective quality only when viewed as a commitment to a sphere beyond and above man. Viktor Frankl explains:

> If meanings and values were just something emerging from the subject himself—that is to say, if they were not something that stems from a sphere beyond man and above man—they would instantly lose their demand quality. They could no longer be real challenges to man, they would never be able to summon him up, to call him forth. If that for the realization of what we are responsible is to keep its obligative quality, then it must be seen in its objective quality.[1]

Values involve a commitment to a "transcendent authority"—God.[2] Carl Jung, as opposed to Freud, points to the fact that a "transcendent authority" is a determi-

---

1. Viktor Frankl, *Psychotherapy and Existentialism* (New York: Simon and Schuster, 1967), p. 64.
2. Viktor Frankl, *The Will to Meaning* (New York: World, 1969), p. 63.

nant in an individual's life and that the human psyche is penetrated with religious feelings and ideas:

> . . . the life of the individual is not determined solely by the ego and its opinions or social factors, but quite as much, if not more, by a transcendent authority. . . . I do not hold myself responsible for the fact that man has, everywhere and always, spontaneously developed religious forms of expression, and that the human psyche from time immemorial has been shot through with religious feelings and ideas. Whoever cannot see this aspect of the human psyche is blind and whoever chooses to explain it away, or to "enlighten" it away, has no sense of reality.[3]

Through values, the transcendent and the holy uplift the human. Such uplift, however, is real only when actions consistent with personal values are done for God and not merely for "good conscience." Frankl maintains:

> A man who is striving for a good conscience in which he can rightly say, "I possess a good conscience," would already represent a case of pharisaism. A really good conscience can never be reached by grasping for it, but solely by doing a deed for the sake of a good cause, or for the sake of the person involved, or for God's sake.[4]

VALUES AND PERSONALITY INTEGRATION

Values are the norms, goals, or purposes that one chooses in order to give a sense of direction and meaning to one's life. They are the integrative forces that bring about the wholeness in one's personality. One evaluates

---

3. Carl Jung, *The Undiscovered Self* (Boston: Little, Brown, 1957), pp. 22-23.
4. Frankl, *Psychotherapy and Existentialism,* p. 41.

self-worth in accordance with one's consistent loyalty to the value system one has freely chosen. Frankl points out that human life is authentic only when it is lived according to personal values:

> . . . being human means being in the face of meaning to fulfill and values to realize. It means living in the polar field of tension established between reality and ideals to materialize. Man lives by ideals and values. Human existence is not authentic unless it is lived in terms of self-transcendence.[5]

Freida Fromm Reichmann considers self-realization as one of the most important therapeutic goals. Its attainment, she believes, is dependent upon established values:

> By "self-realization" I mean a person's use of his talents, skills, and powers to his satisfaction within the realm of his own freely established set of values. Furthermore, I mean the patient's ability to reach out for and to find fulfillment of his needs for satisfaction and security, as far as they can be attained without interfering with the law or the needs of his fellow-men.[6]

Rev. Charles Curran maintains that progress or change in counseling or psychotherapy occurs when there is a "rediscovery of basic values":

> When people change in counseling and psychotherapy, it appears to be not simply because someone has educated them but because they have come to what is often a rediscovery of basic values.[7]

5. Viktor Frankl, *The Will to Meaning* (New York: New American Library, 1970), pp. 51-52.
6. Freida Fromm Reichmann, *Principles of Intensive Psychotherapy* (Chicago: University of Chicago Press, 1971), p. 34.
7. Charles A. Curran, *Counseling and Psychotherapy* (New York: Sheed and Ward, 1968), p. 79.

Values become integrative forces in life only when an individual exercises his or her freedom and responsibility. Value conflicts occur when a person is crippled by the perpetuating compulsion for conformity, when a person lacks the sense of autonomy necessary to make a choice of values or to make any value judgment. The person who fears to take a stand for fear of rejection or ridicule will lead a life of continually conflicting values. Refusing to exercise one's freedom to make choices about values is synonymous with refusing to be responsible. Indeed, habitually irresponsible behavior is one of the signs of disintegrating mental health. Frankl states:

> What man actually needs is not homeostasis, but what I call noödynamics, i.e., that kind of appropriate tension that holds him steadily oriented toward concrete values to be actualized, toward the meaning of his personal existence to be fulfilled. This is also what guarantees and sustains his mental health; escaping from stress situations would even precipitate his falling prey to the existential vacuum.[8]

VALUES AND MATURITY

Adherence to a sense of values is a sign of maturity. A mature person possesses a unified philosophy of life. Curran points to the internalization of "limits and controls":

> . . . growth away from narcissism can be demonstrated by the way any expert performance, even in sports, finally demands careful conformity to limits, i.e., self-discipline and control. Maturity in this sense is to the whole of life what conforming to the rules is to a sport: a highly developed skill. The process of maturity is revealed in the child's development through the social

---

8. Frankl, *Psychotherapy and Existentialism*, p. 68.

activity of play, as he grows in the ability to internalize limits and controls.[9]

Maturity involves an awareness that one's adult behavior has its beginnings in values internalized in childhood. As the individual grows toward adulthood, the process of internalization gives way to responsible choices. Erich Fromm incorporates this process in his set of "beliefs":

> I believe that there are two ways of arriving at the choice of the good. The first is that of duty and obedience to moral commands. . . . The other way is to develop a taste for and a sense of well-being in doing what is good and right. . . .
>
> I believe that to recognize the truth is not primarily a matter of intelligence, but a matter of character. . . .
>
> I believe in freedom, in man's right to be himself, to assert himself. . . .
>
> I believe that one of the most disastrous mistakes in individual and social life consists in being caught in stereotyped alternatives of thinking. . . .[10]

The mature individual is able to establish a hierarchy of values. He or she knows what his or her priorities are and arranges them accordingly. Some persons may consider power or success to be of primary importance, followed by material goods or wealth, self, relationship with God, and relationship with family and others. Other persons may give top priority to their relationship with God while still others may choose wealth. Christ pointed to the importance of an awareness of hierarchy of values when he said:

---

9. Curran, p. 213.

10. Erich Fromm, *Beyond the Chains of Illusion* (New York: Simon and Schuster, 1962), pp. 174-82.

"What profit does he show who gains the whole world and destroys himself in the process?" (Luke 9:25).

Mature persons are able to clarify value conflicts when they happen and to resolve them through priority choices. The Russian novelist-in-exile, Alexander Sholzenitzyn, was confronted by two conflicting values: his fierce love for Russia and his determined loyalty to his personal convictions. He had to leave his country in order to remain true to himself.

The mature individual is aware that the value of the self is based on relationships with a Supreme Being as well as with one's fellow beings. An isolated self is a destructive self. The self takes on meaning only when viewed in relationship to God and to other human selves. Martin Buber expounds these relationships:

> The description of God as a Person is indispensable for everyone who like myself means by "God" not a principle . . . and like myself means by "God" not an idea (although philosophers like Plato at times could hold that he was this): but who rather means by "God," as I do, him who—whatever else he may be—enters into a direct relation with us men in creative, revealing and redeeming acts, and thus makes it possible for us to enter into a direct relation with him. This ground and meaning of our existence constitutes a mutuality, arising again and again, such as can subsist only between persons. The concept of personal being is indeed completely incapable of declaring what God's essential being is, but it is both permitted and necessary to say that God is also a Person. . . . As a Person, God gives personal life, he makes us as persons become capable of meeting with him and with another. But no limitation can come upon him as the absolute Person, either from us or from our relations with one another; in fact we

can dedicate to him not merely our persons but also our relations to one another. The man who turns to him therefore need not turn away from any other I-thou relation; but he properly brings them to him, and lets them be fulfilled "in the face of God."[11]

The mature person is therefore able to experience a real and personal relationship with God—a relationship based on love and trust rather than fear of punishment. The mature person's relationships with others are warm, accepting, and nonjudgmental because they are purified and sanctified in God.

---

11. Martin Buber, *I and Thou*, trans. Ronald Gregor Smith (New York: Scribner's, 1958), pp. 135-36.

Our capacity for joy enables us
to see the comical realities within
us and around us.

VI

JOY AND HUMOR—THE HUMAN
AND THE HOLY EMBRACING LIFE

The capacity for joy and humor is innate in every human being. Joy and humor are the balancing factors that enable the person to perceive life objectively. The individual who has developed his or her capacity for joy and who possesses a keen sense of humor is more able to cope effectively with the stress and strain of life's realities than is the person who is joyless and humorless. Moreover, happy persons who are able to perceive realities with a touch of humor are easier to relate to than moody persons who are compulsive perfectionists.

JOY IN PERSONALITY DEVELOPMENT

The feeling of joy or happiness is evident even in infancy. The infant smiles or expresses joy in relation to its physical well-being as early as the second or third month. Several months later, the baby responds joyfully to tickling. During the second year of a child's life, playing with toys, watching other children play, and experiencing pleasant sounds stimulate the feeling of joy, which is expressed not only in smiles but also in laughter and the clapping of hands. The baby's joy is greatly increased as he or she overcomes obstacles in his or her activities and attempts at success. In early childhood (ages three to six), the sources of joy are many, including physical well-being, incongruous situations, unexpected sounds, and new discoveries. Teasing and playing pranks on children or adults lead to feelings of superiority, which make the child happy. The joy response consists of smiling, laughing, clapping of hands, jumping up and down, or hugging the object or person who elicited the emotion. The child's ability to express joy will depend not only on the intensity of the emotion but also on the social pressures on the child to control it. Some cultures encourage an open and healthy expression of joy while other cultures stress reserve and suppression.[1]

As children grow toward the teen years, their capacity to experience joy is intensified. The sources of joy include physical well-being and pleasant experiences, especially in relationships and material possessions. Gifts become an important stimulus to joy.[2] As the teenager grows toward early and late adulthood, he or she begins to develop an inner sense of joy—the joy that stems from spiritual relationships. This joy includes peace derived from a clear conscience and the spiritual experience of the realness of

---

1. Elizabeth Hurlock, *Developmental Psychology* (New York: McGraw-Hill, 1959), pp. 102, 138-39, and 283.
2. Ibid., pp. 182-83.

God's existence. An individual who is able to maintain this capacity for spiritual joy throughout his or her life possesses a neutralizing force that enables the individual to cope effectively with tragedies and stresses in life. Joy provides the individual with an inner sense of security with which to perceive objectively sources of anxieties in daily life. The capacity for joy does not exclude the realities of existential suffering. The willing acceptance of suffering as it occurs serves to deepen one's capacity for joy. The source of experiential joy is not outside but within the self.

In certain instances, the capacity for joy is crushed in infancy or childhood. A baby separated from his or her mother, a child deprived of affection and cruelly treated by adults, and a teenager continually exposed to humiliation or overpressured to succeed are robbed of the capacity to enjoy life and become imprisoned within the walls of neurosis or emotional disturbance.

THE HAPPY PERSON

A healthy person is able to experience happiness, to function effectively at a job, and to relate satisfactorily with others. A happy person accepts himself or herself unconditionally. Fully aware of his or her potential, gifts, talents, and achievements, a happy person can love and appreciate the person that he or she is. A happy person is aware of personal limitations, failures, and mistakes, which he or she accepts as learning experiences and stepping stones to further progress. In accepting himself or herself, such a person is able to accept God and to develop a personal, meaningful relationship with him. Persons cannot have a healthy relationship with God, much less pray, while they harbor self-contempt or self-hatred. To the degree that they can love themselves, they can also love God.

The happy person is able to accept and handle his or her feelings, including pleasure, joy, anger, guilt, anxiety, and pain, which the person does not suppress but shares with a loved one. The happy person is able to express anger and other negative feelings calmly and constructively, without destroying another person's self-esteem and without destroying his or her relationship with the other.

The happy person is able to enjoy his or her work and to accomplish it efficiently. He or she does not allow work to control him or her, but uses common sense to determine the amount of work he or she can do without undermining his or her health. The happy person is able to find meaning in his or her work and to discover therein an expression of love and service rather than the compulsive means of dealing with frustrations and anxieties.

The happy person is able to control and to integrate thoughts, fantasies, desires, emotions, and behavior. He or she is able to control negative thoughts and fantasies that stimulate unreal anxieties and fears and to curb and channel sexual desires into creative activities or hobbies that give pleasure and satisfaction.

The happy person is able to accept and adapt to change. He or she is fully aware of the reality of change in the universe, in society, in community life, in other people, and in himself or herself. The happy person does not cling to the past but confronts the reality of the here and now. Through his or her accepting attitude toward change, he or she maintains a resiliency that facilitates continual adaptation to changing environment and situations. The happy person is therefore able to accept changes through middle age and, eventually, to grow old with graciousness and gentleness rather than with the crabbiness and bitterness brought about by the refusal to affirm change.

The happy person is responsible for his or her own life, its direction, and the decisions he or she makes from day to day. The happy person deals with his or her commitment to God and fellow human beings with the sincerity that his or her sense of responsibility requires. He or she is honest about his or her ability to keep commitments. The happy person does not blame others for sufferings or miseries, for he or she is able to detect where his or her responsibility lies. He or she has a healthy and objective perception of reality, which facilitates his or her ability to deal with real situations responsively and effectively.

HUMOR—AN OBJECTIVE PERCEPTION

A sense of humor is a human being's safety valve. The capacity to enjoy humorous situations is an indication of an individual's ability to perceive life objectively. Gordon Allport describes the value of humor thus:

> Humor may throw an otherwise intolerable situation into a new and manageable perspective. The neurotic who learns to laugh at himself may be on the way to self-management, perhaps to cure.[3]

A sense of humor enables us to discover the sunny truth of an otherwise grim situation. It helps us to sort out the nonessential or irrelevant in the midst of stress and the pressures of life. Humor produces laughter, which releases tensions of anxiety, anger, or hostility. A person with a

---

3. Gordon Allport, *The Individual and His Religion* (New York: Macmillan, 1950), p. 52.

sense of humor is never a perfectionist, either with himself or herself, with others, or with life itself. Humor stems from the capacity to affirm the humanly imperfect as well as the humanly ridiculous without fear of what others think. An individual with a keen sense of humor can accept the ambiguities and paradoxes of life because he or she is fully aware of his or her ultimate values.

THE DEVELOPMENT OF HUMOR[4]

At four months of age, a baby experiences the comic in vocal play or babbling. He or she finds enjoyment in blowing bubbles in water or in dropping things. When the child is a year old, making funny faces becomes a source of enjoyment. Hiding from adults is another source of amusement as a baby grows older. At the age of two, the baby enjoys stunts like squeezing through a narrow space.

In early childhood (age three to six), the child finds pleasure in teasing and playing pranks on other children as well as on adults. As the child begins to perceive incongruities, slapstick comedy becomes a source of enjoyment and fun. The child's response to humor consists of laughing, clapping of hands, and jumping up and down. The funny antics of pets, as well as grimaces and noises made by the child himself or herself, also become a source of humor.

The child at seven to twelve begins to develop a group sense of humor, playing practical jokes on other children and adults, such as teachers. But at this age humor is not yet fully developed. The child still enjoys the slapstick shared with playmates. As the child grows toward

---

4. Hurlock, pp. 108, 139, 154, 197, and 202.

adolescence, he or she begins to understand jokes and enjoy them. Comical situations also begin to bring amusement and laughter. But only the adult is able to derive humor from unpleasant situations.

HUMOR AND HEALTH

The realities of human life are interwoven with stressful and anxiety-provoking experiences. Needless to say, stress and anxiety take their toll on one's health. Humor helps one cope with unpleasant or frustrating situations. Viktor Frankl associates humor with self-detachment:

> By virtue of self-detachment, man is capable of joking about himself, laughing at himself, and ridiculing his own fears. By virtue of his self-transcendence, he is capable of forgetting himself, giving himself, and reaching out for a meaning of his existence.[5]

Orlo Strunk says that humor is characteristic of a mature person:

> If insight is characteristic of the mature person, so too is humor, which, says Allport, is a correlate of insight. By a sense of humor is meant the ability to laugh at the things one loves and still to love them. Allport calls humor man's principal technique for getting rid of irrelevancies.[6]

In order to develop a sense of humor, a person must accept human nature unconditionally. The perfectionist imposes such idealistic and unrealistic expectations upon himself or herself and upon life itself that he or she is

---

5. Viktor Frankl, *The Unheard Cry for Meaning* (New York: Simon and Schuster, 1978), p. 122.
6. Orlo Strunk, *Mature Religion* (New York: Abingdon Press, 1965), p. 91.

forever complaining or criticizing. Because nothing meets his or her perfect specifications, he or she perpetually finds himself or herself depressed or under stress. The person who accepts the incongruities of life, the blunders and mistakes that inevitably happen, is able to laugh and release tension. He or she is able to look at the brighter side of life and have fun. He or she enjoys laughing at himself or herself, and this laughter helps build up coping resources to deal with stress.

Silvano Arieti supports the healthy influence of humor:

> Various authors have stressed that humor in all its aspects has a healthy influence on the human organism. This influence would again place it close to dreams, which also have salutary physiological and psychological effects. Patricia Keith-Spiegel (1972), summarizing the views of authors ranging from Spencer (1860) and Darwin (1872) to Menon (1931), concludes, "Laughter and humor have been hailed as good for the body because they restore homeostasis, stabilize blood pressure, oxygenate the blood, massage the vital organs, stimulate circulation, facilitate digestion, relax the system, and produce the feeling of well-being."[7]

HUMOR AND WHOLENESS

Humor and sanity go hand in hand. Wholeness of personality enables one to be concretely aware of reality. Reality, however, is a mixture of paradoxes. True humor stems from paradoxical situations. The individual who is keen in perceiving such situations bursts into laughter because the element of the unexpected has caught him off

---

7. Silvano Arieti, *Creativity: The Magic Synthesis* (New York: Basic Books, 1976), p. 123.

guard. Gilbert Keith Chesterton wrote about his perceptions of religion and morality with humorous insights,
which led Hugh Kenner, one of his critics, to write:

> If Chesterton is not, like Eliot in his poetry, creative,
> he is never, like Eliot in his later essays, irresponsible.
> If he cannot practice art in its major sense, as creation,
> he practices it constantly in its broader sense, as mak-
> ing; and what he makes is never trivial: it is always
> geared to his extraordinary metaphysical perception.
> Here, in this less intense form of aesthetic activity, if he
> is not great, he is sane.[8]

A keen sense of humor is indicative of a person's healthy
perception of reality, of his or her ability to discern
spiritual implications in concrete or unpleasant situations.
This capacity to delve into the core of reality is integral not
only to humor but also to mysticism. Chesterton understood this relationship:

> Mysticism keeps men sane. As long as you have
> mystery you have health; when you destroy mystery
> you create morbidity. The ordinary man has always
> been sane, because the ordinary man has always been a
> mystic. He has permitted the twilight. He has always
> had one foot on earth and the other in fairyland. He
> has always left himself free to doubt his gods; but
> (unlike the agnostic of today) free also to believe in
> them. He has always cared more for truth than for con-
> sistency. If he saw two truths that seemed to contradict
> each other, he would take the two truths and the con-
> tradiction along with them. . . . Thus he has always
> believed that there was such a thing as fate, but such a
> thing as free will also. . . . The mystic allows one thing
> to be mysterious and everything else becomes lucid.[9]

8. Hugh Kenner, *Paradox in Chesterton* (New York: Sheed and
Ward, 1947), p. 2.
9. Ibid., pp. 64-65.

The autobiography of the great mystic, St. Teresa of Avila, is sprinkled with humorous insights along with her mystical experiences. There is also humor in the Gospels. Indeed, Christ's parables are humorous perceptions that only mystics who feel secure in themselves and in God are able to understand and enjoy.

Laughter is the offshoot of love. Why does a mother laugh at her child, a husband at his wife, a friend at a friend? Why do we laugh at someone whom we love deeply? Humor and laughter are indications of acceptance, of unconditional love for the other, for love is able to recognize and transcend human limitations, frailties, and inconsistencies.

Sr. Barbara Marie Palicki

Loving and being loved are fulfilling only when we are aware that love's source is divine.

VII

CARITAS AND EROS—UNION OF THE HOLY AND THE HUMAN

Love is life-giving, life-sustaining, and constructive. For Christians, love had its beginning in God, and Christ's teachings center on love as the motivating force in relationships with God and other human beings. Both the Commandments and the Beatitudes protect the individual from self-destruction and the destruction of others because they are grounded in love. The person who cannot love develops destructive tendencies toward self and others. Loving is the function of the spiritual dimension in every human person. Its expression, however, is made possible by the physical dimension. Human behavior is either constructive or destructive; it is indicative of the person's capacity to love or to hate.

CARITAS

The term *caritas* refers to love in the Christian sense, as indicated in the Gospels, in Paul, and in Augustine.

Caritas is the extension of one's self in fellowship with God and one's neighbors. Caritas does not preclude one's sexual identity; it enhances one's identity as a personal relationship is established with God and with other persons. While recognizing sexual needs and desires, Christian love transcends them in order to satisfy spiritual needs. Spiritual hunger in every human being is satisfied only in the attainment of a personal fellowship with God.

Christian love presupposes that the individual has attained a degree of self-love and self-appreciation in order to be able to extend the loving self to God and one's neighbors.

CELIBATE GIFT

The call to the priesthood or the religious life, which had its beginnings in Christianity, is a mystery for each individual so called. Through the centuries this call has proven the capacity of human beings to transcend and sublimate sexual needs. Although celibates can have unconscious motives and be sexually repressed, their conscious goal is the fulfillment of a spiritual need based on Christian values. Persons who pursue religious life or the priesthood because they fear the opposite sex or the responsibilities and anxieties of marriage are living lives of falsehood and hypocrisy that breed only unhappiness and discontent. No matter how lofty or sublime the celibate life style may be, it is destructive to an individual driven by fear, who must discover his or her own real self and work through the masks and escape mechanisms in order to arrive at a point of honest decision making.

Only a healthy and mature person can make a decision in favor of a life style that demands the extension of self to the point of oblation. The authentic celibate's decision is not made under compulsion; nor is the celibate psychologically driven. Authenticity involves freedom to make a deliberate choice based on one's values and convictions.

The authentic celibate is able to make a gift of the self because he or she loves and appreciates himself or herself as a gift from the Creator. The act of giving is the basic expression of love. In order to be able to give, an individual must first be aware of having received, of being loved.

AUTHENTIC CELIBACY AND SEXUALITY

Authenticity in the celibate life does not mean rejecting sexuality or even genitality, which are gifts of human nature. However, each human person has the freedom to choose what to do with these gifts. One can choose fulfillment in family life and genital intimacy or opt for spiritual fulfillment by sublimating the sexual and genital gifts. The French philosopher Jean Guitton, although a layman, aptly describes such sublimation:

> ... sublimation is in no way the renouncement or repudiation of the principle of love; to sublimate is not to deny but to assume; it is not to destroy but to restore upon a higher level; not to condemn but to glorify. . . . Sublimation is a peaceful effort to achieve nature's work in us, that of perpetually raising up the lower by causing it to participate in the higher life.[1]

Yet authentic celibacy can never be fully appreciated by the celibate who has not accepted and understood his or her own sexuality. Like all persons, celibates need intimacy,

---

1. Jean Guitton, *Human Love* (Chicago: Franciscan Herald Press, 1966), p. 91.

but sexual acting out is certainly not the way to meet this need. Self-alienation must be overcome and loneliness must be accepted before intimacy with the self is achieved. Only by being intimate with his or her self can an individual discover his or her capacity for spiritual intimacy—that quality of intimacy that brings about a genuine personal relationship with God and a more meaningful and lasting friendship with other human persons.

Viktor Frankl says that although the need for intimacy can drive a person to sexual promiscuity, it can also offer that person "an opportunity to meditate":

> People cry for intimacy. And this cry for intimacy is so urgent that intimacy is sought at any expense, on any level, ironically even on an impersonal level, namely, on the level of merely sensual intimacy. The cry for intimacy then is converted into the invitation "please touch." And from sensual intimacy it is only one step to sexual promiscuity.
>
> What is needed much more than sexual intimacy is existential privacy. What is greatly needed is to make the best of being lonely, to have the "courage to be" alone. There is also creative loneliness which makes it possible to turn something negative—the absence of people—into something positive—an opportunity to meditate. By using this opportunity one may make up for the industrial society's all to heavy emphasis on the "vita activa," and periodically spend some time on the "vita contemplativa." From this we may see that the real opposite to activity is not passivity but rather receptivity.[2]

Persons can never fully understand sexuality unless they profoundly appreciate their own bodies. Penelope

---

2. Viktor Frankl, *The Unheard Cry for Meaning* (New York: Simon and Schuster, 1978), pp. 71-73.

Washbourne describes the "body awareness" that she believes is essential in attaining personal authenticity:

My body is my possibility and my limitation. To the extent that "I" control "its" actions, I forget that "it" controls "me." We are what we eat and sleep and drink and smoke and exercise and touch. Body awareness . . . that means my being aware of the total organic structure and my being able to feel bodily what it needs. I know the hunger signs, the sleep signs, but do I know the exercise signs, the touch signs? How strange it is that I am an "I," a "person" who has the responsibility to feed my body, wash it, put it to bed: I "decide" what the body needs. I don't know anymore how to listen to its needs or respond to its rhythms.

As a child I was so aware of my body in contact with the new-mown grass, the dampness of it, the glorious smell of it. . . . swimming is marvelous. . . . the feel of water on my skin exhilarates me. Sun warming my skin, wind in my hair. . . . my vivid awareness at the age of eight of the sweet smell of lilacs in bloom, or lying on my back in the grass looking up at the blue sky and seeing white blossoms. . . . all the things that I remember as a child are of intense bodily feelings, of being alive to my body responding to its environment, of delighting in my body as it felt and smelled and tasted and touched.[3]

According to Washbourne, every human person has a "sacred obligation" to his or her own body:

Opening myself to my own body, being responsible to it, caring for it, and creating a situation in which its body-based experiences can be trusted is my most

---

3. Penelope Washbourne, "My Body/My World," in *Male and Female*, ed. Ruth Tiffany Barnhouse and Urban T. Holmes III (New York: The Seabury Press, 1976), p. 88.

sacred obligation to myself. To open myself to myself is the same as opening myself to others. As a child it is through close physical contact and organic relatedness with my parents that I can learn to trust my own body. I must be open, relax into being an organism interconnected with others.[4]

Sexual structures in the body reveal both the human and the holy:

They can reveal to me more about the dark, the demonic, and the fearful than anything else can. They can also show me what the holy means, what ecstasy means, what creation means, what life and death mean, what trust and love mean. In a way nothing else is as clear to me as the experiences of my own body. Theology, God, doctrinal discussions only make sense if I know the ground from which I am speaking. The meaning of life and death, the question of transcendent dimension, the experience of grace become most real on the visceral level, and most particularly so in the experience of my female sexuality.[5]

UNDERSTANDING PSYCHOSEXUAL DEVELOPMENT

For the celibate who is deprived of a healthy understanding of his or her psychosexual development, human sexuality becomes a threatening monster—a perpetual source of guilt or the reason to stifle and crush the capacity to love. Unloving and unlovable virgins are not uncommon; fear of their own sexuality incapacitates them in establishing the wholesome friendships that are indispensable to maintaining a fulfilling celibate life.

---

4. Ibid., pp. 88-89.
5. Ibid., p. 94.

An infant is born with organs indicating gender identity. The organs of the male differ from those of the female. During early childhood (ages three to five), the child becomes curious about his or her body and begins to discover its different parts. The attitude that the child develops toward his or her sexual identity and sexual behavior will depend upon the attitudes of the family. If the mother's attitude is negative, the child will develop fear of or disgust for his or her own body. On the other hand, if the mother's explanations about sexual functions are positive and suited to the child's level of understanding, the child will develop a reverence for his or her body.

Interest in sex increases during late childhood (ages six to twelve), when the child wants to know more about sexual relations and the birth process. If parental attitudes are negativistic and ignore or condemn the child's normal curiosity, the child will manage to obtain information from friends who share stories, jokes, or books about sex. At this stage, sexual exploration or homosexual play occurs. Wise parents take time to acquaint their sons and daughters with changes in their bodies. The girl is prepared by her mother for the coming of her menstrual period, and the boy is given an explanation for nocturnal emissions. Such parental preparation helps the girl and the boy accept without fear and with a sense of security the physical changes soon to occur.

At puberty, the girl or boy becomes aware of sexual feelings. As the interest in sex becomes very strong, the boy or girl tends to fantasize. If parents speak of sex as sinful and immoral, the child may build up guilt feelings, especially about masturbation, and these guilt feelings can create anxiety or scrupulosity that may surface in adulthood or middle age. During this period, parents and teachers can help the child affirm his or her sexual identity by fostering acceptance and respect for the human body. Healthy sexuality will develop only if such affirmation occurs.

Healthy sexuality, moreover, is achieved only when a person has established the right and definite gender identity. Persons enjoy a particular gender role established by their particular cultures. Healthy sexuality requires that persons accept their genitality with a sense of responsibility, not only for its use but also for its abstention. Individuals must make responsible choices for their own well-being and that of others.

Early adolescence (ages thirteen to seventeen) is the period of religious awakening. The adolescent with emotional conflicts is both unhappy and unstable. Unfortunately, this period traditionally was the time when entrance to the seminary or religious life was encouraged. Psychosexual development is not complete at this age. Ordinarily, the adolescent discovers his or her need for closeness with someone other than members of the family. As the adolescent is attracted to the opposite sex, dating becomes a means of establishing these close relationships.

During late adolescence (ages eighteen to twenty), going steady and early marriage are common. At this stage, however, individuals have not yet attained the emotional maturity needed for a stable commitment. Psychosexual development reaches its maturity between ages twenty-one and twenty-eight. Commitment to either celibacy or marriage is more reliable when it is made during this period.

By the time of early adulthood (ages twenty-one to thirty-nine), men and women who have not decided to remain single or to enter religious life or the priesthood are usually married. Celibate men and women may manifest adolescent behavior in early adulthood, especially if they entered the seminary or convent during adolescence. Traditional religious formation did not facilitate emotional growth. Stunted psychosexual development accompanied by ignorance of human sexuality produced immature and insecure personalities for whom guilt and scrupulosity was an obsession. Celibates may "fall in love" homosexually or heterosexually, and, unless professional help is made available, they may develop definite patterns of self-destructive behavior caused by psychosexual immaturity. Thus, during early adulthood, celibates need to be fully aware and accepting of their sexual feelings in order to sublimate them in a healthy manner through wholesome friendships and hobbies in music, arts, and crafts.

Middle age (ages forty to fifty-nine) is a critical period for women. Women experience menopause, or a decrease in the production of hormones by the ovaries. This physical change affects a woman's moods. If earlier stages of her development have been marked by unresolved emotional conflicts, the woman at menopause can be depressed, critical, difficult to please, and irritable. Women who have made healthy adjustments at earlier stages are able to go through menopause calmly and are able to accept hot flashes and other bodily discomforts graciously.

Men also experience a climacteric, although it occurs later for men than for women. If at middle age a man has not achieved the goal or success he set for himself, he may experience a consequent loss of self-esteem or depression. Middle-aged celibates may experience disillusionment and discontent if they have failed to achieve personal goals. Frustrations in relationships with superiors and community members may cause the individual to seek compensation through homosexual or heterosexual affairs outside the community. It is very important for the middle-aged celibate to attain a certain degree of fulfillment within the community and to establish satisfying relationships. Only then will the celibate be able to sublimate effectively the negative manifestations of his or her sexuality. Deprivation of satisfying relationships and anxiety about self-image may drive the celibate to compensate in unhealthy or inappropriate sexual behavior that is inconsistent with his or her commitment.

Old age (sixty until death) is either the golden age or the period of decline, depending on an individual's attitude and mental health. Happiness in old age depends not only on an individual's goal fulfillment but also on how a society or a religious community regards its senior members. In cultures wherein old age is revered as symbolic of wisdom and achievement of goals, elderly men and women experience the peak of a lifetime's satisfaction. But in cultures wherein old age is synonymous with unproductivity and uselessness, this period can be the most tragic stage in one's life.

Bodily changes and ill health affect one's appearance in old age. Mental and physical activities decline, and loss of friends and relatives occurs through death. Depression caused by loneliness seems to be the inevitable consequence of aging. Celibates are fortunate in that they are more attuned to an afterlife. Aging and approaching death do not terrify such persons who have accepted and regarded their sexuality as a sacred gift and who have behaved responsibly in regard to their commitment. Celibates know that even after the body has turned to dust, identity remains.

Human sexuality has its spiritual and physical dimensions that must never be ignored. Their recognition and integration are indispensable to a meaningful life and a happy death.

LOVE—THE SPIRITUAL QUALITY IN EROS

Eros without love is animal function. Love is a human phenomenon, and sex is human only because humans are able to love. Guitton and Frankl both perceive love as extending or transcending self:

> Faust, like Don Juan, does not belong to the category of those who love. To love, one must go forth from oneself, discover and create the other at the same time that one allows oneself to be discovered and created; this supposes equality and reciprocity within sex-differentiation.
>
> Now Faust is too fond of himself to love; he seeks not so much to excite love as to experience his own power which is all the more flattering when innocence is its object. In that he is blood-brother to Don Juan, that desperado, who no longer believes in the power of intoxication to forge an eternal bond with a single being, who makes use therefore, of all love potions and loves as many times as there are nights.[6]
>
> Love is really one aspect of a more encompassing human phenomenon which I have come to call self-transcendence. . . . man is—by virtue of the self-transcendent quality of the human reality—basically concerned with reaching out beyond himself, be it toward a meaning to fulfill, or toward another human being lovingly to encounter.
>
> Loving encounter, however, definitely precludes regarding or using another human being as a mere

---

6. Guitton, pp. 32-33.

means to an end—as a tool for reducing tensions created by libidinal, or aggressive, drives and instincts. This would amount to masturbation, and in fact that is how many of our sexually neurotic patients speak of the way they treat their partners: in fact they often say they "masturbate on their partners." Such an attitude toward a partner is specifically neurotic distortion of human sex.

Human sex is always more than mere sex, and it is more than sex to the extent that it serves as the physical expression of something metasexual, as the physical expression of love.[7]

Love requires maturity. One has to be mature in order to be able to perceive the uniqueness of the other. Frankl describes how a mature person loves:

. . . To the mature person the partner is no "object" at all; the mature person, rather, sees in the partner another subject, another human being, seeing him in his very humanness; and if he really loves . . . he even sees in the partner another person, which means that he sees . . . uniqueness. This uniqueness constitutes the personhood of a human being, and it is only love that enables one person to seize hold of another in this way.

Grasping the uniqueness of a loved one understandably results in a monogamous partnership. The partner is no longer interchangeable. Conversely, if one is not able to love, he winds up with promiscuity.[8]

It is unfortunate, however, that our modern society strips human sex of its spiritual quality and degrades it as a commercial item:

But we should not forget either that the myth of sex for fun's sake as something progressive is promoted by

7. Frankl, pp. 80-81.
8. Ibid., p. 81.

people who know it is good business. What intrigues me is the fact that the young generation not only buys the myth but is blind to the hypocrisy behind it. In an age when hypocrisy in sexual matters is so frowned upon, it is strange that the hypocrisy of those who promulgate a certain freedom from censorship remains unnoticed. Is it so hard to recognize that their real concern is unlimited freedom to make money?[9]

The pleasure principle is in no way a reliable criterion for love. Authentic love is responsible. Eros without responsibility is no longer human. Millions of teenagers receive sex education, but since they lack responsibility and maturity, the result is tragic. Young people need to learn how to love and be responsible before they are introduced to sex education; otherwise, it will lead only to self-destruction and destruction of the other.

MAN AND WOMAN—EQUAL YET DIFFERENT

Western culture is competitive. The male breadwinner competes with other males in the acquisition of material security. Women who are not breadwinners are therefore expected to assume a subordinate or inferior role. Human history has often depicted women as the "possession" of men: as wives or as daughters given away in marriage.

The Gospels, however, reveal Christ's respect for women as equals. Remember the account of the woman caught in adultery, the "sex object" to be destroyed after having been exploited. Granted, Christ's compassion was directed at the punitive group, but that compassion was based on his respect for the woman as a person. Christ was very subtle in pointing to that equality when he said,

---

9. Ibid., p. 82.

"Whichever one of you has commited no sin may throw the first stone at her" (John 8:7). The Samaritan woman's reputation certainly did not make her inferior in the eyes of Christ, who revealed himself to her as the Messiah. Christ's treatment of Mary and Martha of Bethany exemplified his respect and love. The Jewish divorce law, which made it easy for men to repudiate their wives, underscored female inferiority. Christ made women equal with men, and that equality is necessary to human relationship.

Dietrich von Hildebrand mentions the value of the differences between men and women:

> . . . man and woman differ not only in a biological or physiological direction, but that they are two different expressions of human nature.
>
> It is also important to see that this difference has a specifically complementary character. Man and woman are spiritually ordered toward each other; they are created for each other. They have first a mission for each other; second, a much closer communion and more ultimate love is possible between them than between persons of the same sex because of their complementary difference.[10]

He also points to the danger of men becoming "coarse, dried out, or depersonalized" when completely cut off from any contact with women and of women becoming "petty, self-centered, and hypersensitive" when completely isolated from men.[11]

While it is true that the good influence of a woman can bring out the noble qualities in a man, a woman's influence can also be destructive:

10. Dietrich von Hildebrand, *Man and Woman* (Chicago: Franciscan Herald Press, 1966), p. 14.
11. Ibid., p. 15.

Dr. Mary C. Jones, a psychologist, did a follow-up study, covering thirty years, of several hundred children who had been brought up in Oakland, California. Since greatly detailed information was available about the subjects in their childhood, it was possible to single out characteristics peculiar to those who had become alcoholics. The research disclosed that these individuals had indifferent, rejecting mothers and lived in families that lacked warmth and understanding.[12]

Homosexuality, in some instances, can also be traced to the mother:

Although there are a variety of theories as to the causation of early developmental failure, they all have in common severe disturbances in the early child-parent relationship when critical maturational changes are taking place. All the data suggest that a binding and psychologically crushing relationship between a mother and son leads to a later concept of women as potentially dangerous and destructive. The outcome of this type of relationship between a young male child and his mother may result in an excessive clinging to her, anxiety upon attempting emotional separation from her, and a consequent disturbance in masculine identity.[13]

Thus a woman's influence upon the family and the society can never be underestimated. The quality of love a woman bestows upon her husband and on each of her children determines their mental health and happiness.

---

12. Harry Milt, *Alcoholism: Its Causes and Cure* (New York: Scribner's, 1976, p. 40.
13. Charles Socarides, "Homosexuality Is Not Just an Alternative Life Style," in *Male and Female,* ed. Ruth Tiffany Barnhouse and Urban T. Holmes III (New York: The Seabury Press, 1976), p. 145.

To welcome the processes of
aging and death is to bring to
harmony the transitory and the
eternal.

VIII

THE INEVITABLE REALITIES:
AGING AND DEATH—THE TRANSITION
OF THE HUMAN INTO THE HOLY

In spite of their being so reality conscious, modern individuals deny the realities of aging and dying. Because these realities induce fear, denial is the easiest means of handling them. Yet the denial of reality is self-defeating, for the individual thus refuses to prepare for the inevitable. Coping with reality demands that a person first accept reality as such—its inevitability and the loss experienced in the process.

THE PROCESS OF AGING

The aging process starts with birth. From birth on, growth and aging go hand in hand. As the individual goes through different developmental stages, he or she also approaches old age. Chronologically, old age extends from sixty until death. Chronological age, however, is an inaccurate criterion to use in determining the beginning of old

91

age because the symptoms of old age vary markedly among individuals. Getting old affects people differently, and the rate of aging differs between men and women. The process of aging is also influenced by heredity and the conditions affecting the individual during his or her various developmental stages.

MODES OF COPING WITH OLD AGE

Awareness and acceptance of the reality of old age are important factors in coping with it. Old age does not rob an individual of his or her freedom to choose and responsibility for choosing how to deal with his or her condition. Barring brain dysfunction, the individual can choose to be autonomous, to maintain an alert attitude toward life, and to pursue varied interests that stimulate creative activities. An individual can immunize himself or herself against cultural change and adjust to it with flexibility, thereby increasing his or her wisdom. Or an individual can attach himself or herself to a protective environment, which enables him or her to function normally but whereby he or she refuses change. He or she is then able to function well only because the environmental structures provide him or her with the usual security.

An individual also can choose to become or to continue to be overly dependent. But the moment emotional and environmental supports are withdrawn, this choice leads to the deterioration of physical vitality. Because of his or her dependency, the individual is unable to function on his or her own. Physical aging usually precedes mental aging. However, the reverse happens in some individuals when they let go mentally as soon as the signs of aging occur. There is more danger of wearing out from disuse than from enjoyable and sensible activities. Among the great artists who have continued their creative activities through an advanced age are Pablo Casals, who continued to delight his audiences with his cello concerts until he was past ninety; Arthur Fiedler, who still conducts the Boston Pops in his eighties; and the queen of mystery thrillers, Agatha Christie, who continued to write past her eightieth year.

ADJUSTING TO OLD AGE

Self-image plays an important part in successful adjustment to old age. Favorable self-esteem enables the elderly person to cope with the reality of aging. Earlier experiences also influence the quality of adjustment. Good adjustment prior to old age is a prerequisite for a happy old age. The best preparation for old age begins in childhood, when children are taught to accept both pleasant and unpleasant realities. This acceptance provides a solid foundation for making good adjustments in the future when physical and mental resources start to wane. Successful adjustment requires accepting the physical limitations imposed by old age, taking good care of one's health and grooming, detaching oneself gradually from attitudes and behavior that are no longer viable, and continuing to develop interests outside self and the family.

HAPPINESS IN OLD AGE

Since old age is viewed as the period of illnesses, physical dependency, loss of friends and loved ones, and inactivity, it is equated with depression and sadness. Yet the degree of happiness an individual experiences at this time of life depends upon the quality of adjustment. Affirmation of self and affirmation from others are conditions for happiness. The individual needs to be realistic about himself or herself, accepting conditions in self and environment even when they do not meet expectations. During this period in life, the individual also feels very keenly the need for spiritual security as the reality of death comes closer.

Usefulness, freedom from isolation or loneliness, and economic security are elements necessary to an elderly person's happiness. The happier the person is, the more alert and healthy he or she is, the more open and accepting he or she will be of approaching death.

DEATH AS LIFE'S CONCLUSIVE POINT

Elisabeth Kubler-Ross's great contribution to modern society is helping modern man to face the reality of death not only with courage but also with great hope. According to Kubler-Ross, death is the final stage of growth. Her studies on death and dying have confirmed what religion has maintained through the ages: death is a transition to life.

Teilhard de Chardin was not only a man of science; he was a man of deep love and faith. He looked closely into the meaning of death. He commented that "if there were no death, the earth would certainly seem stifling." For him, death is "the only way out to a greater life." Death does not return us to "the great current of things" but "surrenders us totally to God."[1]

---

1. Henri Lubac, *Teilhard de Chardin: The Man and His Meaning*, trans. René Hague (New York: Mentor Omega Books, 1965), p. 109.

FEAR AND DEATH

Fear is the predominant feeling that forces an individual to deny the reality of death. The individual consciously fears the unknown and unconsciously fears punishment. The untrusting, guilt-ridden person is overwhelmed by the thought of death and would rather push it into the farthest recesses of consciousness. One copes with fear only when one is able to find a source of inner security. No human being can give this particular kind of security. Only a Transcendental Being can give man a sense of power over the mystery of death. Thomas Kane points to the healing affirmation that Christ gave to the dying criminal.[2] Because he discovered not only forgiveness but also security in Christ's affirmation, the criminal was able to accept his painful death on the cross. The awareness of a personal relationship with God, the conviction of his presence in the self, gives an individual the confidence to face the death of a loved one and his or her own death. Kubler-Ross cites the greatest lesson learned from her patients, which is also a means of counteracting the fear of death: "LIVE, so you do not have to look back and say: 'God, how I have wasted my life.' "[3]

DEATH AND THE ETERNAL

Death's link with the eternal makes the reality of death awesome. Anthropology's study of funeral rituals and

---

2. Thomas A. Kane, *The Healing Touch of Affirmation* (Whitinsville, MA: Affirmation Books, 1976), p. 32.
3. Elisabeth Kubler-Ross, *Death: The Final Stage of Growth* (Englewood Cliffs, NJ: Prentice-Hall, 1975), p. xix.

burial customs of various peoples and races confirms man's belief in the eternal. Kubler-Ross stresses the importance of keeping the "vision of the eternal" in perspective: "... do not allow the illusory urgencies of the immediate to distract you from the vision of the eternal."[4] Death brings about the transformation God has planned for every human person. As the body dies, the self or the spirit is finally freed from its earthly enclosure to be reunited with the Creator and with loved ones. It is only then that the eternal communion becomes a reality. Teilhard de Chardin's profound understanding of the reality of eternity and communion in death made him write a most insightful prayer:

> O Energy of my Lord, irresistible and living Force, since of us two, You are infinitely stronger, it is for you to consume me in the union that shall fuse us together. Give me, then, something even more precious than the grace which all the faithful beg from you. It is not enough that I die in communion. Teach me communion in dying.[5]

Death is not only the final stage of growth, but also the culmination of the processes involved in the integration of the human and the holy. Death comes as a reward only when the individual has loved and appreciated the gift of life and has exerted effort to integrate the human and the holy within himself or herself.

The rejection of life can never prepare the individual to accept death positively. Suicide is the rejection of life and its realities, of the capacity of the human spirit to transcend pain and suffering. The human is transitory and sub-

---

4. Ibid., p. 167.
5. Lubac, pp. 111-12.

ject to the realities of change as well as misery. It is the holy in the human that transcends transitoriness and anxiety-provoking realities. The holy is the source of integration. It fuses the human and the divine. Death loses its sting only when such a fusion happens in the individual. Only then does death become a happy experience to which we can look forward.

CONCLUSION

It was never God's intention to create man for unhappiness. In every human person there is the insatiable desire to be happy. Freud calls this desire the "pleasure principle." Paradoxically, the frantic effort to attain a state of happiness that gratifies human needs can lead to behavior patterns that bring misery or suffering.

Two forces interact in the human person: grace and human gifts and limitations. I refer to grace as the recognition of God's presence in us. Personality wholeness is possible only when these two forces are appreciated and integrated. It is the rejection of either grace or the human that results in fragmented or confused personality. Affirmation plays a vital role in personality integration. Just as the child needs consistent affirmation from adults in order to develop a healthy personality, the adult needs to be affirmed in order to attain autonomy and emotional stability.

Affirmation implies acceptance and love. The affirming parent or the affirming leader has the capacity to accept and love both the human gifts and limitations of others. Controlling others and imposing one's own expectations on others in the belief that one's action is for the good of the other is an illusion and is, in fact, non-affirming. As the child progresses through the different stages of development, he or she needs to be accepted and loved unconditionally, without unrealistic expectations of perfect or adult behavior. Such expectations stifle emotional growth. The "good" or "perfect" child becomes an adult prematurely, exteriorly. The inevitable consequence of such prematurity manifests itself at mid-life when emotional immaturity gives way to inappropriate behavior and confusion. Non-affirmation of the child's developmental processes and consequent behavior results in deprivation of necessary experiences, including the freedom to make mistakes, which are vital to emotional growth.

The adult should know that emotional growth is an ongoing process to which an adequate degree of self-esteem is indispensable. Only then is the adult able to be true to self, to remain loyal to values and commitments. The self-affirming individual is not crushed by criticisms or by "what others think." He or she is able to accept the past as a stepping stone to further growth. Human sinfulness is not allowed to turn God into a punitive tyrant. Instead, the acceptance of the reality of human propensity to sin intensifies the need for divine mercy and redemption. It deepens compassion for self and for others.

Christ affirmed human nature by his Incarnation. He affirmed human limitations during his Sermon on the Mount and prefaced each beatitude with the words: "Happy are you. . . ." If, indeed, God has destined us to happiness, he also has given us the freedom to affirm that destiny or reject it.